HOW TO MAINTAIN
EYE CONTACT

How to Maintain Eye Contact

poems by

Robert Wood Lynn

Button Publishing Inc.
Minneapolis
2023

◇

Published by Button Poetry / Exploding Pinecone Press
Minneapolis, MN 55403 | http://www.buttonpoetry.com

TABLE OF CONTENTS

HOW TO MAINTAIN EYE CONTACT

IN PRAISE OF LYING TO CHILDREN SPECIFICALLY

Lie to us about our faces getting stuck this way and coffee
stunting our growth and alcohol making more sense

when we're older. Buy us a hamster to teach us about death
but instead teach us that their ears magically change

color every few months. Lie to us and call it an act of love.
Lie to us about an immortal elf that breaks in every December

the way you lie to us about never flirting with our teachers.
Please tell me again about the heaven where

we will all be together again. Even Nana. Even the bank teller
who gave us lollipops every time you made a deposit

and who drove drunk into the bottom of the Rappahannock—
it took days to recover the body—and also the guy on the news

that was vaporized when he tripped and fell into a geyser.
It took less than 24 hours for him to dissolve completely.

He will be in heaven too, which is why it is essential
that you lie to us and keep lying to us. The proximate cause

of everything is eye contact, which is why I have such a hard
time with it. At fault for all of this is looking each other

in the eyes, and maybe touching each other on the arm
just above the elbow, and this you must also lie to us about.

The number one cause of drunk driving is learning to drive
but it's your job to teach us to drive. I met someone yesterday

who looked me in the eyes, even touched me just above
the elbow. I lingered for a second but then I looked away.

I had to. Our faces. Wouldn't it be awful if they got stuck this way?

Part I.
Rehearsals for Being

"It is embarrassing to be alive."

— Mary Ruefle

AT THE COFFEESHOP ON ROGERS

When I was done I took my teacup
to the busing station where the tub said *No Trash*
so, I fished out the teabag, but the only trashcan
had one of those blue liners so I couldn't tell
if it was for recycling. I decided to throw
the teabag out in the garbage on the street
which meant carrying it there, dripping
in my hand like a dead bird, one I didn't kill
but still felt moved to bury—the barista saw
and asked me why, as if a reason was
another license I'd forgotten to renew.
Composting. I said I was desperate
for compost for my garden. Now
every morning she gives me handfuls
of spent teabags the way the cat would
bring me offerings of dead birds,
which seemed sweet until I read how
cats think we can't take care of ourselves.
After being fitted for a hearing aid
my deaf friend was most surprised to find
sunlight didn't hum, was unsettled by how cats
could choose to move in silence. She became
obsessed with the sounds of birds: collective
at first, then individual. Quiet only in repose,
like these teabags I throw away on the street
and feel guilty I don't have a garden. Not even
a balcony. The cat's been dead for years.
It's morning and my hands are soggy, I know,
for the stupidest reason. In spite of the evidence
I am getting good at being alone.

THESE ARE THE RULES
AND THEY HAVE BEEN THE RULES

since before you even thought about being born,
    an action through which you manifested your consent.

You agreed to give foul balls to children under 12 and
    to take photos of tourists when prompted nicely and to curse
      at motorists, but only under your breath.

You agreed to call your mother on all state and federal
    holidays, including the dumb ones.

You agreed to hold doors for strangers even
    the assholes in suits who barge right through.

You agreed to kiss the boo boos of all children that
    ask through stifled tears to make it better,
      and you agreed to believe that it will.

You agreed to kiss every person who goes down on you
    and hard and with grace even if you are still wet on their lips.

You agreed to look for lost dogs on signs
    and you agreed that we are all lost dogs looking for
      each other with a series of signs.

You acknowledged that it will mostly hurt
    and agreed to forget most of it that hurts the most.

You agreed that catcalling is only for cats and
    you agreed to call all cats, but only cats, especially
      late at night in a way that echoes up and down these streets
        like its own kind of sign for lost dogs so that we can find you.

Don't tell me you never asked for this—
  you did a million times by now
     and you do every time you take a breath
      and   there   you just did it again.

I KEEP HAVING THIS FALSE MEMORY

Before the credits finish Nana leans in and whispers that it has
    taken her all her life to realize
that nothing we send the moon is going to calm its man down,
    that no amount of cradling
will ease the anxious expression of bowling balls. I'm going to lose
    her car keys on the way
to the parking lot so neither of us can drive home drunk. We are both
    old enough to know better, probably.

I am old enough to know that feeding the birds when you own cats,
    is just feeding birds to your cats and yet
I told you I loved you—for a moment the cruelest thing to do
    seemed like the nicest thing I could say.
You can't love everything on the food chain the same,
    said my grandfather on his way to the barnyard with a gun
that for the life of me I can't remember was for a fox
    or for the chickens. Seemed like a big distinction at the time

but now I'm not so sure. Everybody is bound to get hungry eventually,
    even the housecats. Especially the housecats.
Maybe after all of this I just need someone to lean in close and tell me
    You are good and I love you
in the voice that everybody reserves for whispering to cats.
    No, not that one, that's the stupid one for babies
and dogs. It's not even a whisper. Quick before the lights come up.
    I want the one for cats.

ON SILENT

after Jamaal May

We used to ring things in this country

                    I was told that we would get to ring things

bells mostly to mark our lives, ourselves

                    on front doors, starts of dinners, ends of shifts

our shaky passage through this bike lane

                    ring out the stale hours, ring in new years

we used to ring things here

                    back when this country was young

you sang into my voicemail with the tone

                    my father used to sound wistful about

manufacturing something lost

                    silence, or maybe that was just

in me, I didn't know what to do

                    when I was young and too noisy to know

so I called my father up to ask

                    what to make of this rust belt of pauses

where the bells used to be

the only expert on silence I know

all he said was *call home more often*

had nothing else to say on the subject, so

I should've known he couldn't help

no one's helped me understand

could you help me make something of

all these ringless moments, silent phones

all this waiting for the train to arrive

all these awful stretches we spend

by ourselves in the quiet of

trying not to throw up, please look for me now

settled snow on a frigid night, breathing

at your front door, exhaling the feeling back

into my slow fingers after texting

I'm here

to you waiting inside

ON ACCOUNT OF GETTING HIS LEG BROKE
BY NEW YORK CITY

cops they gave my friend Carl a *city year* in Rikers some call it
a *bullet* the DA called it a sweetheart deal to keep him away from

all those white supremacists upstate but at sentencing bailiffs made
us leave early when we started hugging told us this is not a wedding

as if we got lost on the way to Our Lady of Perpetual Ignominy and
mistook the twenty-six cops in the courtroom for a choir all of them

staring down the metal-detected crowd it took six hours to visit
Rikers Island for an hour with Carl in the last of five waiting rooms

they had pictures of the Carnegie Hall in Jail program I asked
Carl about it he thought it was a funny joke this is how I learned

even governments say *we used to* to tell stories about what they did
just the once then Carl asked me to send more letters he puts them

under his flimsy mattress for extra padding time was up we got one
hug no one mistook it for a wedding I got back to my phone after all

that to 27 angry emails asking where I was I replied to them
fuck you one by one with the kind of deliberation Carl told me about

no I didn't say *fuck you* I said *I'm sorry I was out of pocket*
it won't happen again it should've but it didn't I want to be that kind

of friend who sends letters I just write them and feel bad about
feeling bad Carl just for you I bought some really soft paper

THIS SIDE OF PARNONAS

I come all the way down to the bottom of this
mountain, Capella, and find only the beginning

of another mountain, as if this descent was a mistake
in need of steep remediation. At the bottom

of the mountain I find you, a donkey named
after a star. Capella, long ago on the subway

in a city you've never been to, I watched
a handsome stranger reading

some thick novel called *The Body Language
of Horses*. He was so graceful sitting there

I went online to buy myself a copy. I found it
wasn't a novel, but an actual guide to the body

language of horses. Listen to me, Capella.
No one should be named after anything

destined to burn out and explode.
Besides, your ears are far too relaxed

to meet that fate. You're no horse, Capella,
but I know a little how to read you. Follow me

back up this hill and I will feed you all the apples
I can steal from breakfast. I will write a book

about the language of donkeys. Capella, imagine
how beautiful the strangers reading us will be.

In New York I invent new kinds of lonely
but here, at least, there is only the one.

Part II.

Rehearsals
for Departures

*"It was discovered the best way to combat
Sadness was to make your sadness a door."*

— Terrance Hayes

ASSATEAGUE

Dropped you off at the airport
for the last again, this time not waiting
around to watch the planes shrug off
this earth. Didn't even pick one to wave at,
to pretend was yours. Abandoned
to my own obsessions, I drove six hours
alone to the island of the wildest ponies
and ignored them. Snow geese, I wanted.
Thick enough to blot the sun. I was younger
then, still under the impression
I could get a year's exercise in a weekend—
that a moment, held right, held always.
So I walked the beach for fourteen hours hoping
to make Maryland and failed. No roads
arrived to take me back. I lay in the sand,
waited for my knees to return. The way you wouldn't
but birds always do. I learned these weren't
the wildest ponies—just the most famous
for being wild. Chubby with salt water, they stood
at a distance disappointing the marsh grass
and the few visitors gathered in the cold.
I had never seen a snow goose before
the day I saw ten-thousand. Their collective static
on the inlet, lifting and landing and
lifting again. Seen one since? I imagine
you asking. No. I mean, maybe once or twice
in passing, though why would it matter?

PRAYER FOR MR. ARMAND PALAKIKO

Not long after dawn on Thanksgiving 2011 at the
Honolulu International Airport,
where it is summer pretty much all of the time,
Mr. Armand Palakiko,
a man whose only job it was to do the futile

work of running stray birds away from runways,
arrived to find a snowy owl
perched on a sign on Runway 8L, a white
apparition out of place from
the tundra, an envoy sent from another time or

maybe just lost. And Mr. Armand Palakiko knew all
birds larger than a fist can
bring down an airplane and so partly for its
own good, and mostly for
the airports', Mr. Armand Palakiko set about charging

the owl with his white Dodge Ram pickup truck
and bombarding it with
firecrackers and nets and couldn't help but feel
silly while chasing around
an arctic bird in the tropics with firecrackers

and nets. But feeling silly while scaring the shit,
white shit, out of birds is
much of the holy work of protecting the
machines of flight and
those of us inside those humming metal wombs,

and there are only so many options, especially
               on the morning of
Thanksgiving, nestled between the busiest flying
               days of the year. And,
having never seen one of these creatures before,

because this was the first in the whole history
               of Hawaii, after having
spent the better part of a shift battling a bird
               braver than fireworks
that crossed the Pacific Ocean a thousand-no,

a million miles from home, and who stayed by
               some magic specifically
just out of reach of all things, all things except
               the shotgun loaded with
birdshot which Mr. Armand Palakiko kept on the seat

of his truck, and what happened next was printed
               in the *New York Times.*
What happened next was that the bird and Mr.
               Armand Palakiko sat down
together around a makeshift table in the bed of

the white Dodge Ram pickup truck by the runway
               overlooking Pearl Harbor,
where we swore we would never again be caught
               off guard by a flying visitor
from far away, so Mr. Armand Palakiko said *aloha,* which

can mean hello and goodbye at the same time, and
               they shared a meal of
Polynesian rats and pumpkin pie and then the owl
               perched on the shoulder
of Mr. Armand Palakiko and whispered the jokes that his

great granddaddy Palakiko used to tell that Mr. Armand
          Palakiko only part way
knew from his father's garbled misrememberings
               and what happened
next was the giving of thanks for the broken down

joy of sharing something so remarkable, so straight
          out of time, and right
now somewhere up in heaven great granddaddy
               Palakiko has the sole job
of keeping god's runways clear of runaway souls

but that is not what it said in the *New York Times*
          when it said what
happened next because what happened next
               was that he shot it.
The first one ever in the whole state and he shot it.

ON MY WAY HOME FROM THE HOSPITAL

Cold night after a long day looking after
my tenses, careful. Late December, though
not late enough to turn this drizzle to snow.
In the glow outside the ShopRite, this lady
in a puffy coat puts, is putting, is trying to put
a twenty-dollar bill back in her wallet, easy
thing made hard by gloves and the envelope
she clenches in her mouth. She misses.
The twenty hits the ground. She bends
to pick it up, it blows away. Windy
though not that windy. It sort of tumbles.
She bends down again; it flits out
of grasp twice over, never stopping more
than a second or two, like a songbird in a bush
moves to keep itself alive. Our lady follows
the bill along the sidewalk stretching to step
on it in spite her bundling. She's running now
as best she can down the gentle slope, stomp.
Miss, stomp again. She's dropping things:
the envelope first. Then her purse, now
her coat. She starts to shriek, maybe with
laughter, maybe fear. And me here, a loss
for how to help her without looking a thief.
All of a sudden, she stops, turns to check
behind, then whirls around again as if trying
to take the damn thing by surprise though
by now it has skittered to the edge of the street,
almost into traffic. The seriousness of her
situation seizes her—this is twenty whole
dollars—so she jumps, two feet coming
down together on the bill. Sticks the landing.
She brings her arms down by her side
in triumph. The crowd erupts. There aren't so many

of us but we clap, bring her belongings to her,
like flowers for a gymnast. Someone drapes
her coat on her shoulders, a medal she's won.
I spent my whole day watching someone
I love die—I mean someone I loved.

HEARTS IS A CARD GAME FOR EXACTLY FOUR PEOPLE

And I am one of them, you used to say, along with
    Nothing ruins a game of Hearts like a fifth friend,
which is how we learned better than to make one.
    Hearts was also how we learned panic as an art form

and the hopeful noise our problems let out while gliding
    down on other people. Oh, Amir playing so conservative
while I dumped diamonds early to make myself a ghost.
    How you sought the two of clubs like a speaking conch.

Remember Patrick trying to shoot the moon with every
    hand? Collecting each discarded heart as if
it was a precious thing, the way an old woman fishes
    soda cans from the subway tracks with a hook on a string.

His suicide pact with the Queen of Spades, the kind
    of scheme that never works until it never needs to again.
Yes, Patrick and the moon—it really was every single hand,
    a thing equal parts endearing and infuriating. Same as his

mash-shuffle. Same as the grin he wore out doing it. Same as
    the way he put all his money into bitcoin then evaporated
into cryptic message board dispatches from all over the world,
    posted under a handle we have never been sure is his.

Turns out nothing ruins a game of Hearts like losing
    your fourth friend. You said *Hearts is a card game*
for *exactly four people* and we are none of them.

POEM ENDING IN A PUBLIC SERVICE ANNOUNCEMENT

The year I resolved to be
      one of those people who washes

their car on the weekends I didn't
      have a car, so I settled

for fresh flowers on the table,
      six dollars a week. *Cheaper*

than cigarettes but won't kill
      anybody, my friend put it

between exhales. But what use is that
      to a non-smoker? So I tried

coughing my way through
      the porches of bars. It didn't take—

in those days nothing did,
      not even the names of the colors

shrugging petals under my kitchen
      window. Only the tiger lilies

that came so close to poisoning
      my cats. In the Hall of My Fears,

the first room is devoted
      to how casually we can kill

what we love without noticing.
      The vet bill was fourteen

hundred dollars. We all lived
      long enough to learn the etymology

of *antidote*: Greek for *give against*.
      I'm always embarrassed

how cats are the only way I've managed
      to mark time. Define myself

by what I keep alive or don't. To think,
      I gave them flowers, gave this poem

antidote as a metaphor.   No wait—
      forget all that. If you're going to remember

any part of this: *Don't buy lilies if you keep
      cats.* Their kidneys, I'm telling you.

Lilies fuck up their kidneys.

ALL THE WAY DOWN

I stood by myself so long the silence got loud, kinda how
if you go far enough south it's not even the South anymore:

you're Miami. I lived there once, sweated free the LeBron
years drinking breakfast with other people's tios. All of us

waiting for the ocean to take us with it. None of us conceding
to keep cereal in the fridge. In west Kendall, backed up against

the national park, I was sure the world was over. And three
miles in, that it hadn't ever begun. Whenever I got like this

I would go to the part of the Everglades called Shark Valley
which I liked because it was also a liar. Flat as ocean

with nowhere for nothing to swim. I'd walk hours, evaporating
its little road through the sawgrass till the gators blocked

the path back. Nothing to do but wait for them to move,
not unless I wanted to get eaten. This is how I knew I didn't.

I'd stand there in the not wanting it. The silence all screaming.

THE HEARTBEAT HYPOTHESIS

As it turns out there is this silly trick to knowing how long you,
    no anybody, no any creature, will live:
divide the average lifespan of an animal by its metabolic rate

and you'll get a number that is about one billion. That's what we get,
    about one billion heartbeats on this planet.
One billion, a magic enough number & if physics has struggled,

struggles & in all likelihood will continue to struggle forever to find
    its unifying equation, here is biology's—the kind
of surprise you trip over because it's just been sitting there all along

like a golden retriever on shag carpeting, one already most of the way
    through her billion & where she is joined by the blue
whale & the field mouse, each given one billion beats on Earth

unless someone or something intervenes & quiet now you can hear it
    tick ticking away, your billion ticking like the kind
of clock they mostly don't make anymore & once I believed that

in every clock there were tiny creatures moving the parts & now
    I cannot help but know inside of these creatures
there are more parts marching even faster to the same number

onebillion onebillion onebillion & it can drive you mad, even
    billionaires go mad, cartoonishly mad, for
the one thing they cannot buy: more heartbeats, & they sit in a tube

someplace air-conditioned in Arizona, their rhythm frozen while
    animated mice power the clocks & calculators
that keep this math like a metronome: terrible,   free.

Part III.

Rehearsals for Apocalypse

"And death with a top hat
quietly laughing at us as he passed.
Even that we will miss. Even that we loved."

— Steve Scafidi

ON WEDNESDAY THEY CAME ON THE NEWS

to finally admit that the planet is burning up.
All the ice has broken and as a result
there are no such things as strangers anymore.
Or polar bears, but that's not the point.
All the ice has broken and now there are
no strangers. Now there is no such thing as
polite silence in an elevator. Now you say hello
to every single person on the street as you
swim past. Sure, this means we are all going
to die—that was always going to happen—
but more importantly there is no ice left to break.
The planet has doffed its polar caps to us
like a gentleman in a silent movie and suddenly
we do the same to everyone that gets on the bus,
only louder, and tell them our favorite jokes,
even the off-color ones, because what's a dirty joke
among friends when the apocalypse is coming
prematurely? *Sounds like my husband*,
says the reference librarian, unbuttoning her collar
to let out a little of this steam. All the ice has broken
and so there are no more quiet cars on trains,
no concept of small talk. All of it melted away,
and now in an effort to save the few trees
we have left we cut the word *oversharing*
from our dictionaries. There is only *sharing*,
so we do that, over and over. This planet
is overheating and where I expected riots, a run
on the grocery stores, and maybe roving bands
of thieves, I found instead just a bunch of my friends,
seven billion of them. We all grew up on Earth
together, back in the day, back when there was ice.
(Yeah man, remember ice?) Anyway,

those guys, I love them. All the ice has broken
and they are just texting to say *Hello, I miss you.*
You look hot today, so hot. Positively on fire.

AFTER ALL THE UNPLEASANTNESS, ARMS HAVE SOMETHING TO SAY FOR THEMSELVES

Anyone who told you we were here to toss fists
here to get pointy over armrests here to push people

off of barstools or over tables even sometimes
into traffic anyone who says that deserves exactly

what we gave them we didn't ask for this we asked
you to remember us jutting out in front of loved ones

just before they walk into the street remember us thrown
like seatbelts across the passenger side remember

us lifting lovers onto kitchen counters to let tongues
do their holy work remember every time we've reached

over to brush hair out of a friend's face so you can look
them in the eyes how we tossed nieces just high enough

they never doubted we'd catch them please remember us
slung over the shoulders of friends leaving a party

at sunrise while the legs teeter and mouths round down
the corners of words sung loudly to each other

a few inches away remember us still here holding another steady
steady saying goodbye remember us the engine of the wave

OPPORTUNITY

There would be more mornings, more
dark pink of sun through closed eyelids.
More people rolling over to check
that the other was still there. The day they left
the rover alone on Mars, most didn't read
the news and most of those who did
didn't read about the rover—a wandering
machine supposed to last for only ninety days.
But ninety days passed and still there were more
mornings. People continued to wake up
startled, to churn their way through the covers
to find someone. Some never did, in beds too big
or apartments too small. There were more
mornings for the rover too—thousands more—
until everyone who wasn't a computer
lost count, until the rover made mornings
the wrong metric altogether. Back then,

those thousand days ago, you'd wake up
grasping for me in a panic that felt new
each time. Morning always the same dark pink
that Mars looks in that selfie the rover took
just before it stopped responding.
I'm sorry, I love you always
the first things you'd say aloud
until I stopped hearing the comma.
Not something you needed me to know
so much as a ping sent to a wandering
machine worlds away, still listening
for who knows how long.

INSCRIPTION FOR THE SURFACE OF THE MOON

Hello this is America we invented
human flight & getting bored

of going to the moon we had the idea
for the lightbulb & so it appeared

over all our heads like an anvil
then we invented the television

the infomercial clapping
it on & clapping it off

which means we invented asking
to be slapped during sex

& then the lights all coming
on we invented the supermarket

& having no place to stand
in one without being in the way

we invented stores so large
we had to invent cell phones

to find each other inside
we invented so many kinds

of embarrassment invented
making a name a profile

invented deleting it & sure
we didn't invent sadness but the blues

oughta count we invented sex
lying & lying about sex if we didn't

invent sex there was a time
that rock & roll looked the same

in silhouette besides we invented
the telephone so tell us

who invented phone sex
say it again but slower

you can tell us we didn't invent death
but we're not gonna wait around

for the world's most
careful bomb to disagree

so no we didn't invent
perfection but a man in Texas

named Goodenough invented
the lithium-ion battery

we didn't invent loneliness
only seeing ourselves

in the black screen after
our battery dies mid-conversation

we invented the internet
the direct message & the slide to get there

we didn't invent remembering
how another tastes

just how we tell them about it
desperate & immediate

the only part that counts
good enough or almost so

the way just looking
at this moon will have to do

AT THE END OF BEFORE

We were halal carts in the bike lanes and we were
    bikes on the sidewalk.
We were cats sleeping under parked cars and parks sipping
    from the shower beer
of the East River. We were joy, or at least, no one
    marked joy absent
during roll call. We were strangers on the train
    making friends and we were
the mercy of friends on the train pretending
    not to see each other.
We were the long sadness of having and we were
    having had it just about
up to here. We were people sleeping and
    sleeping people waking
to texts that asked *u up?* We were sex and the hot
    embarrassment of being
but also being together one last time without knowing
    it was the last time.
We were making plans we had no intention
    of keeping and we were
all this tiresome keeping, of time and house
    and secrets and calm.
Forgive us, someone gave us all this to give away
    and still we tried
to keep it for ourselves. We were all this
    and my father's way
of answering the phone *Is everything all right?*
    We were everything, all right.

AFTER

What few of us remain have resolved to get it right
this time, to remake this dirty sphere

into someplace that only loves bullets
in the bodies of emails. Maybe not even emails.

No more emails actually. And this time the only thing
punishable by death will be promises

made between lovers—not their breaking, just
the promises themselves.

And this time instead of a gavel, the solemn theater
of litigation will start with sixty seconds

of looking each other in the eyes without speaking
from a distance close enough to kiss.

Here, all this space saved by getting rid of gavels we can fill
with the open palms of forgiveness. We'll need them

to dig ourselves out of this layer of ash that's buried
everything alive so that we can set up

the cell phone towers again, and test our apologies
on all the things that they can touch.

We'll shoot *I'm so sorry* texts to the servers, to the satellites,
to the hydroelectric dams whirring back to life

because this time it will be understood from the beginning
that apologies are the third highest form of art

after poems and drunk texting your friends how much
you love them. You can kiss me

if you want to, but if asked, I owe you nothing.
Say otherwise, we're goners.

THE MUSEUM OF MAINTENANCE

Retainers, the first thing abandoned. Then vitamins,
weeding. Exfoliating creams. Here, someone dumped
the cakes they'd stopped baking for birthdays, for new
neighbors. There, the cat someone else stopped taking
to the vet. Down the hall of skipped breakfast, church,
and reasonable bedtimes. Around the corner, giving up
on flossing, defragging hard drives. The bathroom
is back there, just past the exhibit of the end of peeing right
after sex. The diorama of the last time some shy someone
asked, *did you come?* No one seems to remember
but there was a time before we let our checkbooks go
all tilty. Gave up calling old friends for new addresses,
the last excuse not to lose them. Upstairs, you can hear it—
what it was before everyone agreed to let smoke alarms pip
until the batteries slept. Now everybody else can too
and we do. By the end we checked bicycle brakes
by sending our children down the steepest hills. Gauged oil
levels with flames from the engine. I couldn't tell you
when it happened, no. By then, we had reason
to quit keeping diaries. By then, we let the future burn
its fossil fuel of the plausibly deniable. Careful to leave
the past leaking, hungry with possibility.

AS ALWAYS

on the first   not quite warm day of March   the park filled
with the delusion of spring   our friends napped   by the half
dozen against a tree   their dogs gathered loose   bikini tops
from sunbathers   made maenads by 53°   we gave time away
in handfuls to the ducks greedying the shore   pairs of men emerged
from winter to wave lures at the water   an excuse to love each other
without looking   as for me I read your cheekbones   their anger
at how I got more time than you   before the good earth was over
fed you grapes   the closest I could get to an apology for something
I didn't choose   then someone at our tree   and very high asked
Is this the Golden Hour?   the light answered   with yellow silence
the way it does   all questions so obvious   later walking you home
I told the story   how my parents fell in love   first drunk   again
sober   only after I existed   I didn't think you were listening
until the moment you stopped   mid-path   mid-sentence
a   way of making me turn around   you told me   *There isn't time
to do anything twice   How come?*   you let the light give
its yellow answer   *I don't want the world to end* you said   okay
but when it does   I will remember it this way   the sun
picking mulch   from your backlit hair   your fresh burnt
shoulders making the gesture   for *All this?*   and *I give up*
at the same time   this last first day   before the good earth was done

RADIO STATIC

it turns out, is just an echo
of the Big Bang.

Ask a scientist. I did
and it's at least half

true, and the other half
she's tired of explaining.

Instead we listened, let lines
crackle. In what passed—

like us—for nothing,
a beginning for all things.

AGAIN WE INTERRUPT THE DISHES

The rinsing of one another's spoons. In this path worn
by all lesser chores, we will trace our scamper
to the park. The bedroom. Bars dark enough
for friends to hold us unembarrassed
by the shoulders. We will make records
of affection, rare things as necessary
as they are unreachable if asked for. And again
they'll sing, our friends, straight into our mouths.
And again, we'll let summer draw us
a field precisely for tossing an apple
back and forth, forth and back, until perfect—
far too bruised to eat. The way we did the day
I learned I loved you. Your joy is an airship
tied to earth by the prospect of its absence. And you
discovered mine ballasted by the dead
weight of the past. Faithful, how morning
will return us to these foamy cups, our plates
half scrubbed. Their ring around the sink.
And even that, a language written for us.
Even that, a way of holding.

Acknowledgements

Versions of certain poems in this book have appeared in the following journals:

Bat City Review: "On Silent"

The Cincinnati Review: "Assateague"

Michigan Quarterly Review: "On Account of Getting His Leg Broke by New York City"

Natural Bridge: "I Keep Having this False Memory"

New Limestone Review: "These Are the Rules and They Have Been the Rules"

New Ohio Review: "As Always," "At the Coffeeshop on Rogers," and "The Heartbeat Hypothesis"

The Penn Review: "In Praise of Lying to Children Specifically" and "On Wednesday They Came on the News"

Rattle: "Prayer for Mr. Armand Palakiko"

Shenandoah: "On the Way Home from the Hospital"

The Southern Review: "The Museum of Maintenance"

Thank you Sam Van Cook and the editors and staff of Button Poetry for your support and belief in my poems over the years. Thank you TaneshaNicole Tyler for your hard work and eternal patience bringing this chapbook to life. Thanks to the Academy of American Poets, the University of Mary Washington, New York University, the James Merrill House, the Stavros Niarchos Foundation, and the Leopardi Writing Conference whose generous support have allowed my writing to develop. Thank you to my friends and family who make it all possible. Thank you to the faculty and students of New York University's Writers' House—I am deeply grateful to Catherine Barnett, Terrance Hayes, and Deborah Landau for their close readings of so many poems in this text.

About the Author

Robert Wood Lynn is the author of *Mothman Apologia* (Yale University Press 2022), selected by Rae Armantrout as the winner of the 2021 Yale Series of Younger Poets prize. His poems have recently appeared in *The Cincinnati Review*, *Narrative Magazine*, *Shenandoah*, *The Southern Review* and other journals. He splits his time between Brooklyn, New York and Rockbridge County, Virginia.

OTHER BOOKS BY BUTTON POETRY

If you enjoyed this book, please consider checking out some of our others, below. Readers like you allow us to keep broadcasting and publishing. Thank you!

Desireé Dallagiacomo, *SINK*
Dave Harris, *Patricide*
Michael Lee, *The Only Worlds We Know*
Raych Jackson, *Even the Saints Audition*
Brenna Twohy, *Swallowtail*
Porsha Olayiwola, *i shimmer sometimes, too*
Jared Singer, *Forgive Yourself These Tiny Acts of Self-Destruction*
Adam Falkner, *The Willies*
George Abraham, *Birthright*
Omar Holmon, *We Were All Someone Else Yesterday*
Rachel Wiley, *Fat Girl Finishing School*
Bianca Phipps, *crown noble*
Natasha T. Miller, *Butcher*
Kevin Kantor, *Please Come Off-Book*
Ollie Schminkey, *Dead Dad Jokes*
Reagan Myers, *Afterwards*
L.E. Bowman, *What I Learned From the Trees*
Patrick Roche, *A Socially Acceptable Breakdown*
Rachel Wiley, *Revenge Body*
Ebony Stewart, *BloodFresh*
Ebony Stewart, *Home.Girl.Hood.*
Kyle Tran Mhyre, *Not A Lot of Reasons to Sing, but Enough*
Steven Willis, *A Peculiar People*
Topaz Winters, *So, Stranger*
Siaara Freeman, *Urbanshee*
Junious "Jay" Ward, *Composition*
Darius Simpson, *Never Catch Me*
Blythe Baird, *Sweet, Young, & Worried*

Available at buttonpoetry.com/shop and more!

FORTHCOMING BOOKS BY BUTTON POETRY

Mwende "FreeQuency" Katwiwa, *Becoming//Black*
Usman Hameedi, *We Plan On Staying Right Here*
Matt Mason, *Rock Stars*
Anita Dias, *Sitcom Material*

BUTTON POETRY BEST SELLERS

Neil Hilborn, *Our Numbered Days*
Hanif Abdurraqib, *The Crown Ain't Worth Much*
Sabrina Benaim, *Depression & Other Magic Tricks*
Rudy Francisco, *Helium*
Rachel Wiley, *Nothing Is Okay*
Neil Hilborn, *The Future*
Phil Kaye, *Date & Time*
Andrea Gibson, *Lord of the Butterflies*
Blythe Baird, *If My Body Could Speak*
Andrea Gibson, *You Better Be Lightning*

Available at buttonpoetry.com/shop and more!